Animals in Hiding

Contents

Written by Charlotte Guillain

What is camouflage?

Animals use camouflage to hide. Camouflage makes animals look like the place where they hide.

Some animals use camouflage to hunt other animals. Other animals use camouflage to hide from hunters!

Camouflage in the sea

Stonefish look like rocks. They hide to catch other fish.

4

Flatfish look like the seabed. They hide from bigger fish and sharks in the sand.

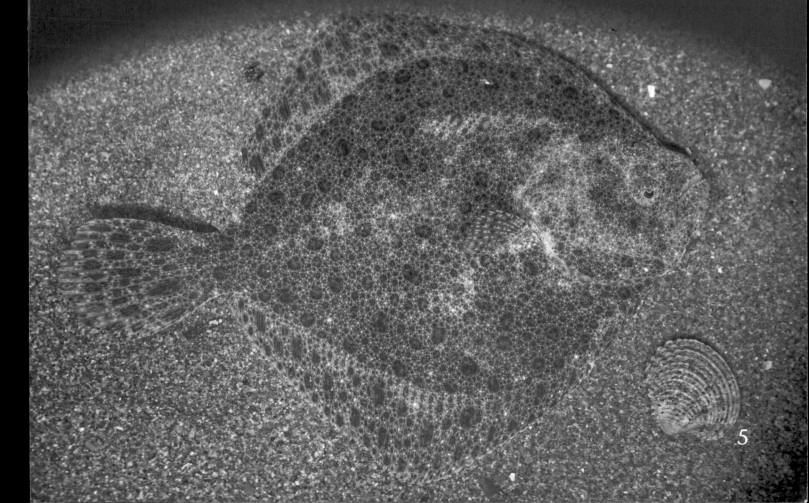

A polar bear's white fur looks like snow.
It can hide as it hunts.

This baby seal's white fur hides it from polar bears in the snow.

Camouflage in grass

A lion's brown fur looks like long grass.
It can creep up on animals as it hunts.

Baby cheetahs' spotty fur hides them from lions in long grass.

This snake's patterned skin looks like leaves.
It hides to catch small animals.

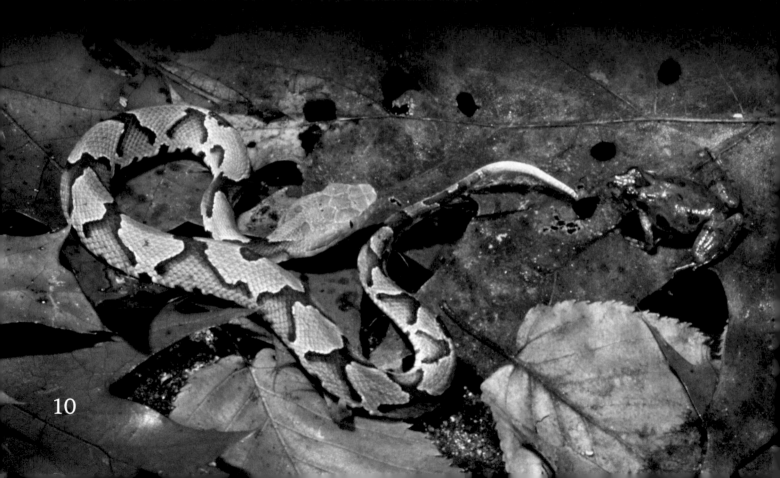

10

This lizard's tail looks like a leaf to hide it from birds and snakes.

Colour change!

This spider changes colour as it hunts insects so they don't see it coming.

Cuttlefish can change colour to hide from sharks.
Changing colour is the best camouflage of all!

Animal camouflage

14

colour

colour change

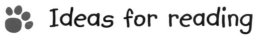 Ideas for reading

Written by Clare Dowdall, PhD
Lecturer and Primary Literacy Consultant

Learning objectives: use syntax and context when reading for meaning; read more challenging texts which can be decoded using their acquired phonic knowledge and skills, along with automatic recognition of high frequency words; find specific information in simple texts; distinguish fiction and non-fiction texts and the different purposes for reading them; ask and answer questions, make relevant contributions, offer suggestions and take turns

Curriculum links: Art

High frequency words: very, how, why, here, use, place, where, other, animals, don't, coming

Interest words: camouflage, stonefish, flatfish, sharks, polar bear, lion's, cheetahs', snake's, patterned, lizard's, spider, insects, cuttlefish, colour

Resources: paper, crayons or paint, high frequency word flashcards

Word count: 162

Getting started

- Play a reading game using flashcards of some key high frequency words, e.g. how, why, here. Dwell on words that children are struggling with and suggest ways to remember them.

- Ask children to read the title and the blurb aloud and look at the front and back covers. Ask children how the frog and seal have hidden, and why they need to do this.

- Turn to the contents page. Ask children to find the word *camouflage*. Discuss how to read the word using phonics as one strategy and noticing less easy sections, e.g. c-a-m-*ou*-f-l-age.

- Explain what the word means if necessary, e.g. how they might wear brown clothes or paint their faces with muddy marks to hide in the woods.

Reading and responding

- Help children to read through the contents page, reading the word *camouflage* with increasing fluency. Discuss what kind of creatures might feature in each chapter.

- Turn to pp2–3. Ask children to read the text with a partner. Remind them that longer words can be tackled using different strategies, e.g. *animals* can be sounded out and blended; *hunters* contains the familiar word pattern *er*.